Reading with Ricky
Ants, Crabs, and Squirrels

Stories by Kathy Kranking
Illustrations by Christian Slade

Contents

2	Lions and Tigers and Ants
10	Learn More: Ants By the Numbers
12	The Haunted Beach
20	Learn More: Look Who's Crabby!
22	The Uninvited Guest
30	Learn More: Squirrels

Lions and Tigers and Ants

It was a hot summer day, and something special was happening at Flora Skunk's house. Flora and her little brother, Sammy, were making ice cream! They were outside at their picnic table. On the table was an ice-cream-making machine. A big cup of liquid was next to the machine.

"Now," said Flora, "we pour this mixture of cream and sugar into the ice-cream maker. Then we turn the crank to make it into yummy ice cream!"

"I scream, you scream, we all scream for ice cream!" shouted Sammy. He was jumping up and down with excitement. Suddenly he bumped into the table, knocking over the cup. The creamy mix spilled all over the table and dripped onto the ground.

"Oh, no!" cried Sammy. "Now what will we do? We won't be able to make our ice cream!"

FLORA WONDERS

Have you ever made ice cream?

"Don't worry," said Flora. "We have more cream and sugar. We can mix up another batch."

Just then, Ricky Raccoon and Bizzie Beaver came up. "Where's the ice cream?" asked Bizzie, licking his lips.

"We had a little accident," said Flora. "So it will take a little longer than we planned."

"That's OK," Ricky said. "Bizzie and I will go do something else and come back later."

Ricky and Bizzie headed off toward Sunny Meadow.

"Hi, guys," said a voice. On a nearby bush, they saw their friend Mrs. Cardinal.

"Hi, Mrs. C," said Ricky and Bizzie.

"We're looking for something to do," said Bizzie.

Mrs. C thought a minute. "You know," she said, "the meadow is a good place to go on a safari."

"We can't go on a safari," said Ricky. "That's something you do in Africa."

BIZZIE WANTS TO KNOW

What do you think we'll find on safari?

"You can find lions and zebras and even tigers right here in the meadow!" said Mrs. C.

"Yikes!" said Bizzie.

"Don't worry," said Mrs. C with a chuckle. "It's perfectly safe. Good luck!" Then she flew off.

Ricky and Bizzie sat down among some flowers. "What do you think Mrs. C meant?" Bizzie asked.

Ricky picked a flower and sniffed it. "I don't know," he said. Then his eyes grew wide. "Hey," Ricky said with excitement. "This flower is a dandelion. A dande-LION!"

"I get it!" said Bizzie. "Now we need to find a tiger and a zebra."

The two friends looked around. They saw butterflies flitting from flower to flower.

"Bizzie, that black-and-white butterfly is a ZEBRA swallowtail," said Ricky.

"And look over here," said Bizzie, pointing out a yellow butterfly with black stripes. "That butterfly is a TIGER swallowtail!"

Ricky laughed. "Mrs. C was right. The meadow IS a great place for a safari!"

Just then, Bizzie's stomach growled. "I'm hungry!" he said. "Let's head back to Flora's place."

"We can go on an ice-cream safari!" said Ricky with a giggle.

Ricky and Bizzie headed back. After a while, Ricky pointed at the path. "Look at that ant," he said. "He's going the same way we are."

Ricky and Bizzie crouched down and watched the little ant scurrying along.

"I wonder where the ant is going," said Bizzie.

Then they noticed more ants. "Look, those ants are walking in a line," said Ricky.

"And now our ant has joined them!" added Bizzie. "Let's see where this ant parade is going."

Ricky and Bizzie followed the ants. They were so busy watching them that they didn't see where they were until they bumped into Flora's picnic table!

"Hi, guys," said Flora. "You're just in time for ice cream."

Sammy crouched down. "What are you doing?" he asked.

"We're following these ants," Ricky said. "And now I see where they were going!" The line of ants ended at the puddle of spilled ice-cream mix.

"That's funny," Ricky said. "The ants were on an ice-cream safari, just like we were!"

RICKY ASKS

Why were the ants marching toward the ice cream?

LEARN MORE

Ants
By the Numbers

2 Ants have two antennas (an-TEN-uhz).

head

6 Ants have six legs.

thorax

abdomen

3

Ants have three body parts.

11

The Haunted Beach

There was excitement in Deep Green Wood. Mrs. Cardinal was planning a surprise for Ricky Raccoon, Bizzie Beaver, Flora Skunk, and Mitzi Mink.

"I can't wait to find out what it is!" said Flora.

"Whatever it is, it will be worth the wait," said Ricky. "Mrs. C always has great surprises."

The day dragged on, until finally, after lunch, Mrs. C appeared.

"Come on, everyone," she said. "Your surprise is ready!"

The friends followed her to a clearing. Mrs. C landed on a branch as the friends stopped in front of a big pile of things. There was a bag, a backpack, and a picnic basket.

"This is the surprise!" said Mrs. C. "You're going to go camping—at the beach!"

Well, a camping trip was exciting enough, but the idea of camping at the beach brought whoops and hollers from the happy gang.

"Thank you, Mrs. C!" they all shouted, high-fiving and hugging each other.

"This should be everything you need," said Mrs. C. "Go on ahead, and I'll meet you later."

Mrs. C waved a wing, and as she flew off she said, "By the way, the beach is haunted." And then she was gone.

At those words the friends all froze and stood looking at each other with wide eyes.

"D-d-did she say 'haunted'?" Bizzie asked.

"Yes," said Flora. "What do you think she means?"

Ricky put on his brave face. "I guess we'll find out," he said. "Let's go." The friends gathered up everything and headed off.

By late afternoon, they had reached the beach. Bizzie hid behind Flora, peeking around. "Do you see any ghosts?" he asked.

"No," said Ricky. "I think Mrs. C must have been kidding."

"Let's play in the water!" Mitzi shouted.

Dropping their things on the sandy beach, they all ran down to the sparkling waves and had fun playing in the water.

After a while, they headed back to their things. "Let's set up our campsite," said Ricky.

Bizzie was already unzipping the big bag Mrs. C had given them. "Cool!" he said. "It's a tent!"

Once the tent was set up, Flora said, "Let's make a campfire. There's a lot of driftwood around here we can use."

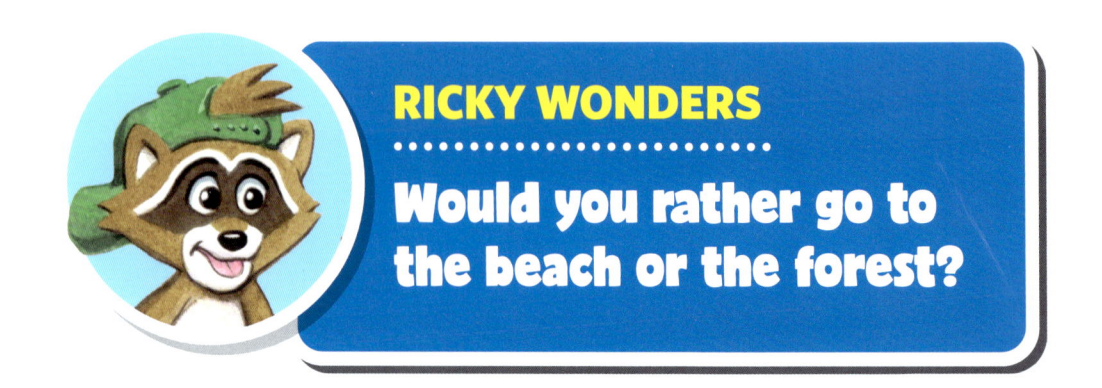

RICKY WONDERS

Would you rather go to the beach or the forest?

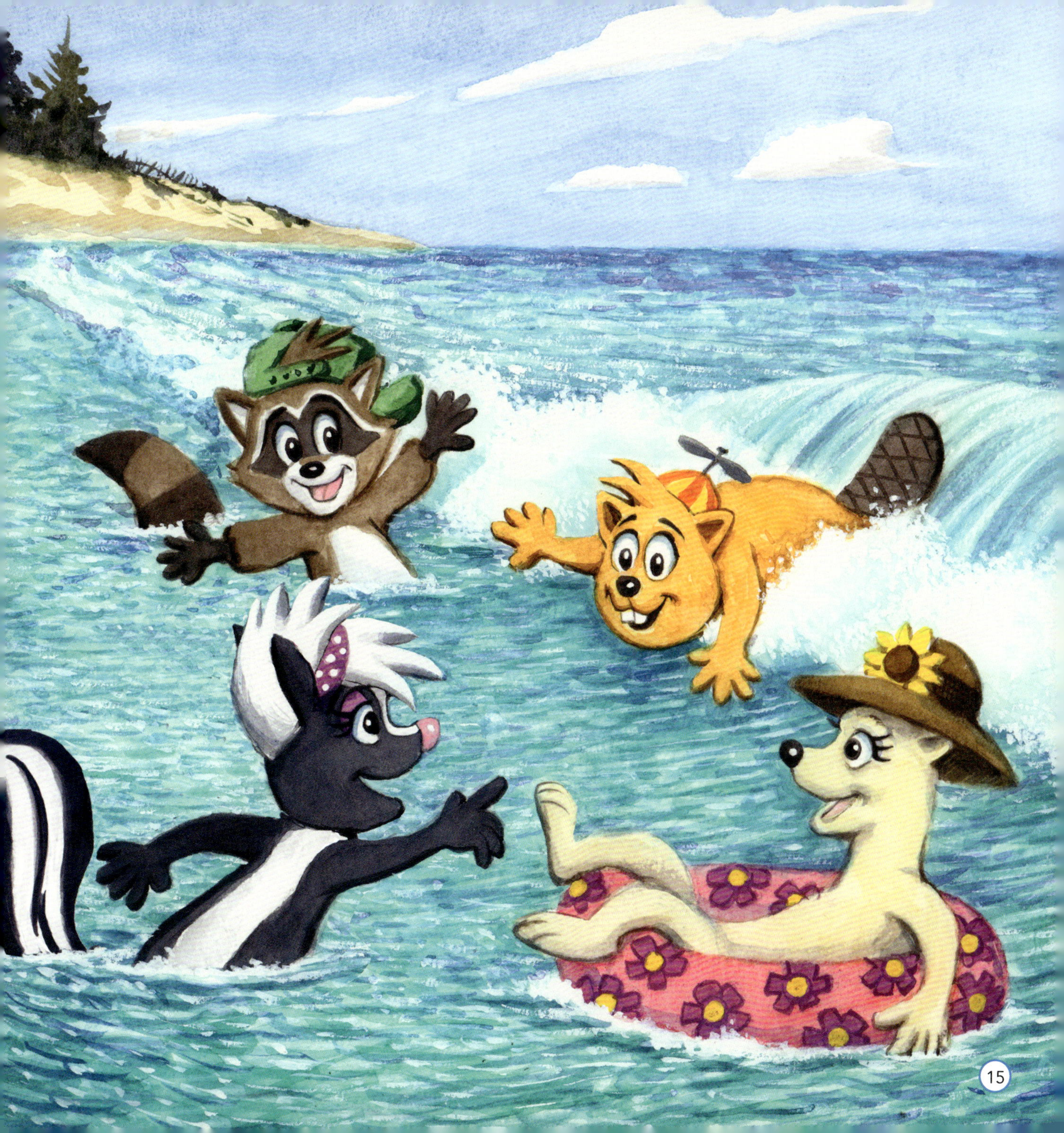

The friends gathered pieces of wood and piled them together. "Does anyone know how to start a fire?" asked Mitzi.

"I can help with that," said a familiar voice, as Mrs. C came flying up.

Soon everyone gathered around a cozy campfire. The sun was setting, and the sky was red and orange.

Flora peeked into the picnic basket. "Mmmm—marshmallows!" she said. "You thought of everything, Mrs. C." Soon the gang was toasting marshmallows over the fire.

After a while, Bizzie peeked into the backpack. "What are these for?" he asked, pulling out some flashlights.

"Oh," said Mrs. C, "those are for our ghost hunt."

Bizzie dropped the flashlights, and the others all stared at Mrs. C. "They should be coming out about now," she said. "Grab the flashlights, and let's go."

The friends nervously followed Mrs. C. It was dark now, and they needed the flashlights to see.

"Um, Mrs. C," said Bizzie. "Why would we want to find ghosts?"

FLORA ASKS

Do you think we will find ghosts?

"Ghosts are scary!" added Mitzi.

"Not these ghosts," said Mrs. C with a smile. She pointed with her wing. In the glow of their flashlights, the friends could see shapes moving across the sand.

Mitzi looked closer. "They're crabs!" she said.

"They're so cute," said Flora. "They run sideways!"

"They're called ghost crabs," explained Mrs. C. "They come out of their burrows at night to look for food. I knew you'd like them."

The four friends stood happily watching the little crabs scurry back and forth.

"This beach *is* haunted," said Ricky, "by really cool ghosts!"

BIZZIE WANTS TO KNOW

Do you think ghost crabs are scary?

19

LEARN MORE

All crabs have ten legs, but not all crabs are the same.

LOOK WHO'S CRABBY!

A **ghost crab** scurries across the rocky shore in search of food.

An **arrow crab** has super skinny legs. It looks more like a spider than a crab.

A tiny **pom-pom crab** holds stinging sea creatures called anemones (uh-NEM-uh-neez) in its claws. The crab uses the anemonies to sting its enemies.

The Uninvited Guest

On a chilly, snowy day, Ricky Raccoon and his friends Flora Skunk, Mitzi Mink, and Bizzie Beaver were having some winter fun. They had spent the morning building snowmen. Then they had a snowball fight. And now they were filling their bird feeders.

"I brought sunflower seeds," said Ricky.

"And I have thistle seeds," said Flora.

"The birds will love these peanuts," Mitzi said.

"Mine's a mix of all kinds of seeds," added Bizzie.

"The birds are going to love them all," Ricky said. He poured his seeds into one of the feeders. But the seeds didn't even fill half of the feeder tube.

FLORA WANTS TO KNOW

Have you ever put out a bird feeder?

23

"That's funny," Ricky said. "I thought I had more birdseed. I think there's another bag at home. I'll be right back." Ricky dashed off.

When Ricky got home and picked up the other bag of seed, he heard the sound of something spilling. He looked down and saw sunflower seeds on the floor. Then he looked at the corner of the bag. A hole had been chewed into the plastic.

"Hey," said Ricky. "Someone's been eating my birdseed! Who could it be?"

Ricky cleaned up the seeds, grabbed the bag, and ran back to his friends.

By the time Ricky got back, his friends had finished filling their feeders. Some hungry birds were already landing on nearby branches, including their friend Mrs. Cardinal.

"Guess what?" Ricky said as he ran up. "Someone went into my house and stole birdseed out of this bag!"

"That's weird," said Bizzie.

Ricky filled the feeder with seeds. Mrs. C and her friends flew to the feeders and began gobbling. "Hmmm," said Mrs. C between bites. "Sounds like you have an uninvited guest, Ricky!"

"Yes," said Flora. "But who?"

The four friends left the birds to their meals, and each headed home. When Ricky entered his house, he looked around for his uninvited guest. "Anybody here?" he asked.

Ricky peeked into the corners and under some furniture. But no one was there. With a shrug, Ricky sat down in his chair.

"Argghhh!" he shouted suddenly, jumping back up. He looked to see what he had sat on. It was a pile of sunflower seed shells. "Someone's been sitting in my chair!" Ricky said.

Ricky cleaned up all the shells. Then he yawned a big yawn. "I'm tired," he said. "I think I'll go to sleep."

Ricky got up and headed for his bed. He dove under the covers. Then he got a surprise. His bed felt crunchy!

"Huh?" Ricky asked, as he threw back the covers. He couldn't believe what he saw. It was a nest of leaves!

"Someone's been sleeping in my bed!" Ricky said. "This is crazy!"

It was clear that someone else felt right at home at Ricky's house. And Ricky was going to find out who it was. So he sat down in his chair and waited. And waited. And waited.

Suddenly, just as Ricky was about to fall asleep, he heard a scratching sound. He jerked awake and listened.

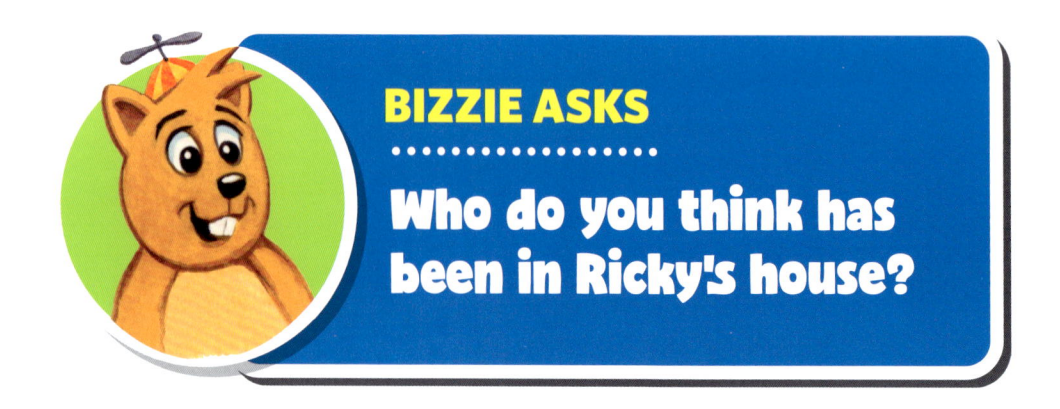

BIZZIE ASKS

Who do you think has been in Ricky's house?

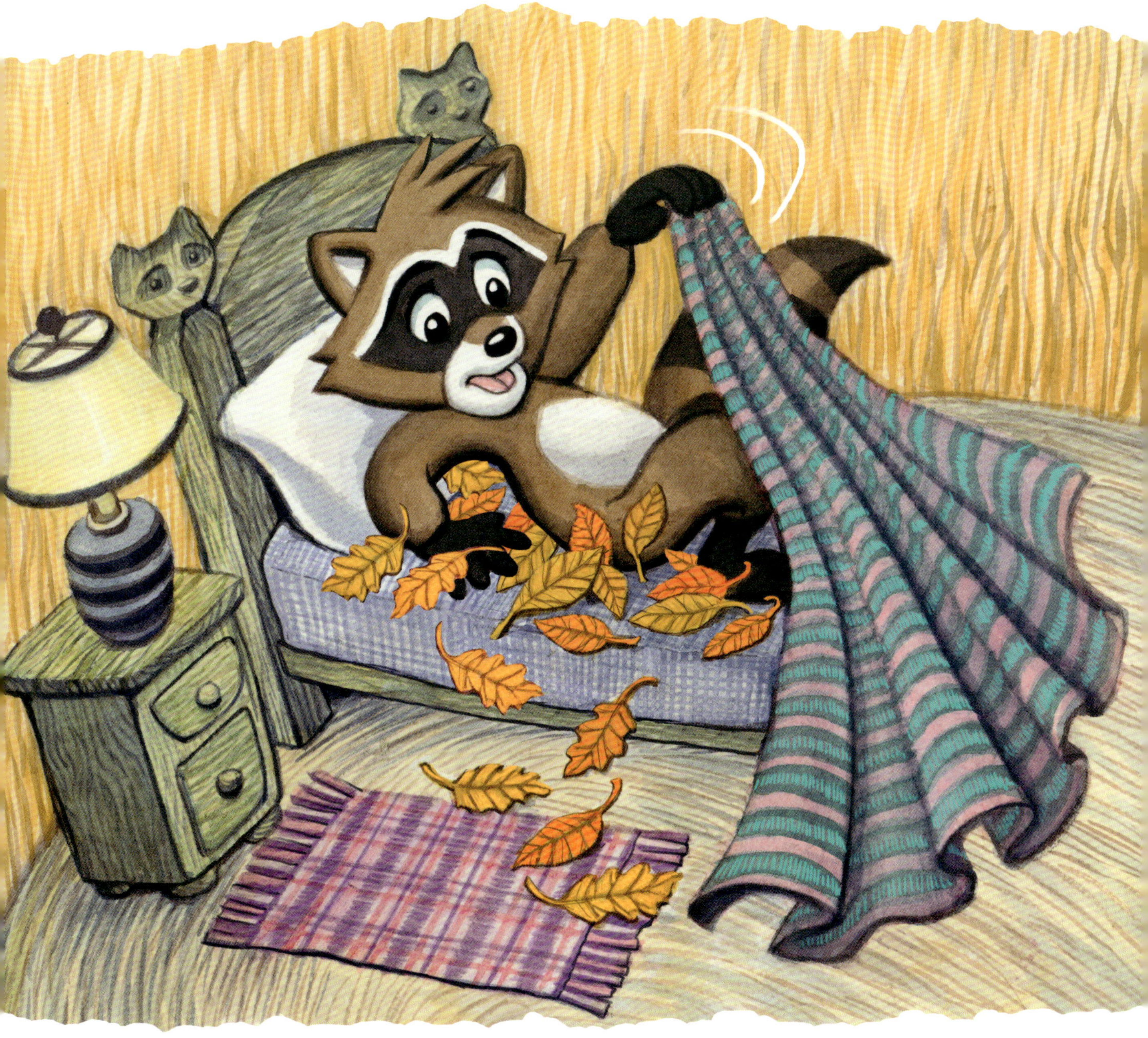

The sound seemed to be coming from the outside of Ricky's oak tree home. It was getting closer. Ricky realized that someone was climbing up the tree. And in another second, a squirrel was climbing in through the open window.

Ricky gasped. The squirrel froze and looked at him with big eyes.

"This is my house," said Ricky. "Sorry, but you can't live here."

The squirrel blinked, then it turned around. And with a flick of its tail, the squirrel disappeared.

The next morning, Ricky told his friends what had happened.

"I guess that squirrel was as surprised as you were!" said Mitzi.

"Yup," Ricky said. "And from now on, the only 'someone' eating my food, sitting in my chair, and sleeping in my bed will be ME!"

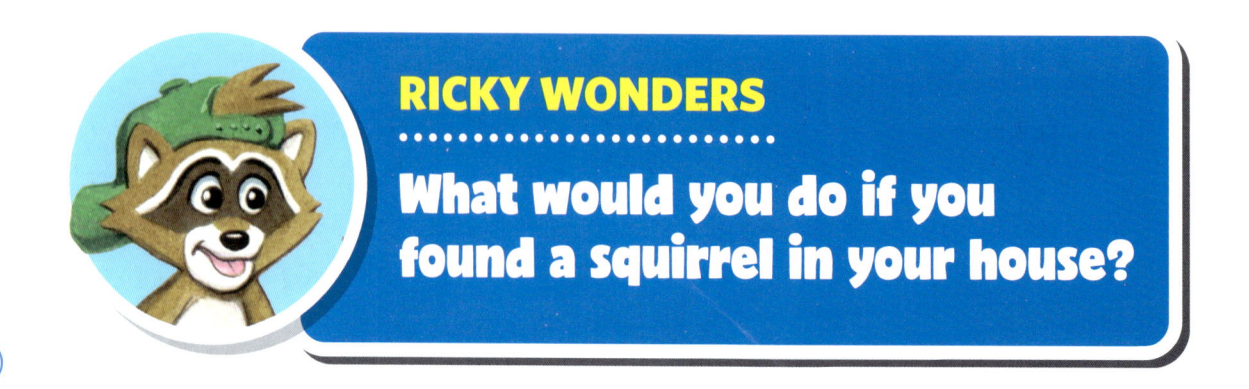

RICKY WONDERS

What would you do if you found a squirrel in your house?

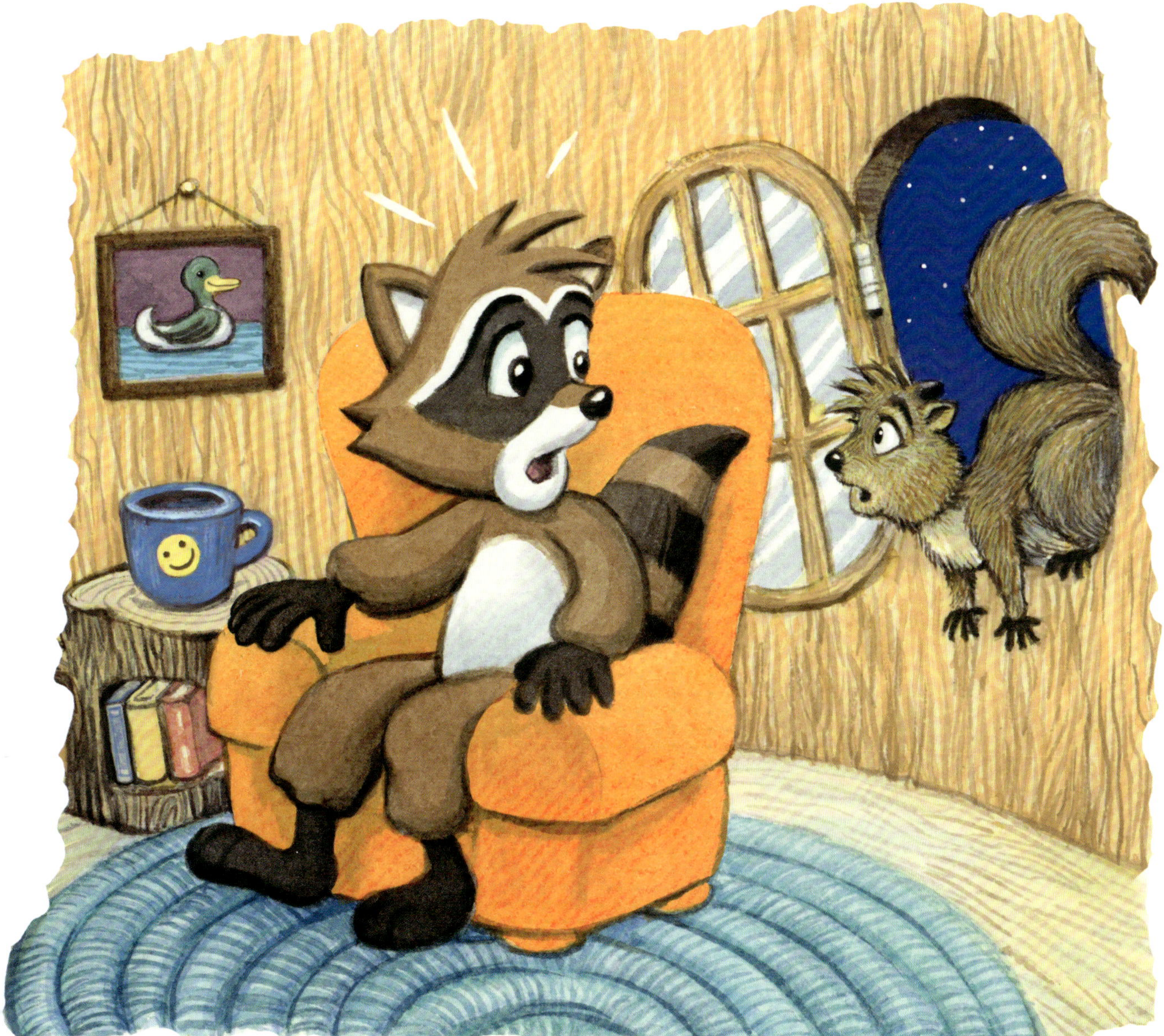

LEARN MORE

SQUIRRELS

By Jennifer Bové

30

We scurry and jump from branch to branch,
Racing up trees and down.
Our claws help us hold onto the bark.
We are the best tree-climbers around!

We really like to climb oak trees.
They grow acorns we can eat.
We crunch the shells with our sharp front teeth,
And the seeds inside are a treat.

Even squirrels get tired of squirreling around
At the end of a long, busy day.
So we sleep in nests of leaves and twigs.
A squirrel's nest is called a drey.

Published by the National Wildlife Federation.

"Ricky and Pals" originally appeared in RANGER RICK JR, a publication for children ages 4–7 in the Ranger Rick family of magazines.

Kathy Kranking, Author
Christian Slade, Illustrator
Molly Woods, Reading Consultant

Photo and Illustration Credits:
Pages 10–11: Hugues de Cherisey / Biosphoto / Minden Pictures; Page 20: Michael S. Nolan / Blue Planet Archive; Page 21: Reinhard Dirscherl / Robert Harding (top), Alex Mustard / NaturePL (bottom); Page 30: Jacky Parker; Page 31: Stephen Dalton / Minden Pictures.

Copyright © 2021 by the National Wildlife Federation.

All rights reserved. No part of this book may be reproduced in any form or by electronic or mechanical means, including information storage and retrieval systems, without written permission from the publisher, except by a reviewer who may quote passages in a review.

Printed in the United States of America.

RangerRick.org

ISBN: 978-1-947254-29-9